This journal belongs to:

_____

Notes

Notes

Weekly Plans & Goals

Week of: _____

	Plans	Goals
Monday		
Tuesday		
Wednesday		
Thursday		
Friday		
Weekend		

Notes

Notes

Weekly Plans & Goals

Week of: _____

	Plans	Goals
Monday		
Tuesday		
Wednesday		
Thursday		
Friday		
Weekend		

The key to success is starting before you are ready

Weekly Plans & Goals

Week of: _____

	Plans	Goals
Monday		
Tuesday		
Wednesday		
Thursday		
Friday		
Weekend		

Notes

Notes

Weekly Plans & Goals

Week of: _____

	Plans	Goals
Monday		
Tuesday		
Wednesday		
Thursday		
Friday		
Weekend		

Be focused.
Be persistent.
Never quit.

Weekly Plans & Goals

Week of: _____

	Plans	Goals
Monday		
Tuesday		
Wednesday		
Thursday		
Friday		
Weekend		

Notes

Notes

Weekly Plans & Goals

Week of: _____

	Plans	Goals
Monday		
Tuesday		
Wednesday		
Thursday		
Friday		
Weekend		

Success doesn't come to you.. you have to go and get it

Weekly Plans & Goals

Week of: _____

	Plans	Goals
Monday		
Tuesday		
Wednesday		
Thursday		
Friday		
Weekend		

Notes

Notes

Weekly Plans & Goals

Week of: _____

	Plans	Goals
Monday		
Tuesday		
Wednesday		
Thursday		
Friday		
Weekend		

Focus on the step in front of you, not the whole staircase

Weekly Plans & Goals

Week of: _____

	Plans	Goals
Monday		
Tuesday		
Wednesday		
Thursday		
Friday		
Weekend		

Notes

Notes

Weekly Plans & Goals

Week of: _____

	Plans	Goals
Monday		
Tuesday		
Wednesday		
Thursday		
Friday		
Weekend		

Work hard in silence
and let your success be
the noise

Weekly Plans & Goals

Week of: _____

	Plans	Goals
Monday		
Tuesday		
Wednesday		
Thursday		
Friday		
Weekend		

Notes

Notes

Weekly Plans & Goals

Week of: _____

	Plans	Goals
Monday		
Tuesday		
Wednesday		
Thursday		
Friday		
Weekend		

Success doesn't come from what you do occasionally, it comes from what you do consistently

Weekly Plans & Goals

Week of: _____

	Plans	Goals
Monday		
Tuesday		
Wednesday		
Thursday		
Friday		
Weekend		

Notes

Notes

Weekly Plans & Goals

Week of: _____

	Plans	Goals
Monday		
Tuesday		
Wednesday		
Thursday		
Friday		
Weekend		

Make a plan.
Write it down.
Work on it daily.

Weekly Plans & Goals

Week of: _____

	Plans	Goals
Monday		
Tuesday		
Wednesday		
Thursday		
Friday		
Weekend		

Notes

Notes

Weekly Plans & Goals

Week of: _____

	Plans	Goals
Monday		
Tuesday		
Wednesday		
Thursday		
Friday		
Weekend		

If the plan doesn't
work, change the plan
but never the goal

Notes

Notes

Notes

Notes

Action is the
fundamental key to all
success

Notes

One day or day one.
You decide

Notes

Notes

Notes

Notes

Notes

Notes

Notes

Notes

Notes

Notes

Notes

Notes

Notes

Notes

Notes

Notes

Notes

Notes

Notes

Notes

Notes

Notes

Notes

Notes

Notes

Notes

Notes

Notes

Notes

Notes

Notes

Notes

Notes

Notes

Notes

Notes

Notes

Notes

Notes

Notes

Notes

Notes

Notes

Notes

Notes

Notes

Notes

Notes

Notes

Notes

www.ingramcontent.com/pod-product-compliance
Lightning Source LLC
LaVergne TN
LVHW012030060526
838201LV00061B/4541